REMEMBER...

THE HIV VIRUS CANNOT BE TRANSMITTED THROUGH SHAKING HANDS, HUGGING, TOUCHING, KISSING, PETTING COUGHING, SNEEZING, SWIMMING POOLS AND TOILETS, EATING UTENSILS OR FOOD, SHARING BEDS, BED LINEN AND CLOTHES, OR THROUGH MOSQUITO BITES.

THE HIV VIRUS IS TRANSMITTED (PASSED FROM ONE PERSON TO ANOTHER) THROUGH THE EXCHANGE OF HIV-INFECTED BODY FLUIDS THROUGH:
- UNPROTECTED (WITHOUT A CONDOM) SEXUAL INTERCOURSE WITH SOMEONE WHO IS INFECTED
- UNSTERILISED EQUIPMENT, INCLUDING NEEDLES, SYRINGES, RAZOR BLADES AND OTHERS THAT HAVE BEEN PREVIOUSLY USED BY SOMEONE WHO IS INFECTED.
- TRANSFUSION OF INFECTED BLOOD OR BLOOD PRODUCTS THAT CONTAIN THE HIV VIRUS.
- AN INFECTED MOTHER TO HER CHILD DURING PREGNANCY, AT CHILDBIRTH OR THROUGH BREAST-FEEDING.

EVERYONE HAS A RIGHT TO INFORMATION, INCLUDING HIV/AIDS RELATED INFORMATION. WE NEED TO BE INFORMED AND SPEAK OPENLY ABOUT HIV/AIDS TO PREVENT INFECTION AND TO HELP THOSE ALREADY INFECTED.

PEOPLE LIVING WITH HIV/AIDS HAVE A RIGHT TO BE TREATED WITH RESPECT AND DIGNITY. YOU SHOULD TREAT PERSONS LIVING WITH HIV/AIDS LIKE EVERYONE ELSE.

FREEDOM FROM DISCRIMINATION FOR ANY REASON (RACE, COLOUR, SEX OR RELIGION, THE OPINIONS YOU HAVE, WHERE YOU COME FROM, WHETHER YOU ARE HEALTHY OR ILL, AND WHATEVER YOUR SEXUAL CHOICES) IS A HUMAN RIGHT THAT EVERYONE SHOULD ENJOY AND ALL SHOULD RESPECT.

ALL GOVERNMENTS ARE RESPONSIBLE TO PROMOTE AND PROTECT HUMAN RIGHTS. GOVERNMENTS SHOULD NOT DISCRIMINATE.

PEOPLE LIVING WITH HIV CAN HELP EVERYONE BETTER UNDERSTAND HIV AND AIDS AND NOT BE FRIGHTENED OF IT, THEY CAN HELP OTHERS TAKE STEPS TO PROTECT THEMSELVES AND THEIR LOVED ONES.

DISCRIMINATION IS WRONG AND UNFAIR. IT IS A VIOLATION OF ANOTHER PERSON'S RIGHT. THOSE WHO DISCRIMINATE SHOULD BE HELD RESPONSIBLE FOR THEIR ACTIONS...

STAND UP FOR HUMAN RIGHTS, TAKE ACTION AGAINST HIV/AIDS DISCRIMINATION! YOU CAN MAKE THINGS HAPPEN!..